Active Kids

Kathryn Smithyman & Bobbie Kalman

Photographs by Marc Crabtree

 Crabtree Publishing Company

www.crabtreebooks.com

KidPower
HEALTHY LIFESTYLES FOR KIDS

Created by Bobbie Kalman

Dedicated by Kathryn Smithyman
For Ethan, who is a bundle of joy

Editor-in-Chief
Bobbie Kalman

Writing team
Kathryn Smithyman
Bobbie Kalman

Editorial director
Niki Walker

Editors
Rebecca Sjonger
Amanda Bishop

Copy editor
Molly Aloian

Art director
Robert MacGregor

Design
Samantha Crabtree
Mike Golka
Heather Caldwell

Production coordinator
Heather Fitzpatrick

Photo research
Crystal Foxton

Special thanks to
Steve Cruickshanks, David Kanters, Heather Fitzpatrick, Sophie Izikson,
Adam Vok, Ivor Selimović, Sunčana Selimović, Alexis Gaddishaw,
Sara Paton, Alfredo Gomez, Erica Olarte, Julio Murch, Sabrina Giancaterino,
William Frampton, Tyler Hendry, Mike Armstrong, Caroline Cheung,
Georgia Desjardins, Alex Fraser, Kevin Murphy, Kelly Bartok, Jonathan King,
Candace Dickson, Kelsey Dickson, Shawn Pellizari, Jenna Stamp, and
Ridley College

Photographs
All photographs by Marc Crabtree except the following:
Bobbie Kalman: front cover & title page (letter "V"), back cover (left),
    page 5 (bottom-left), 6 (top), 7 (top), 8 (center), 9 (right-middle),
    10 (right), 12 (middle), 13 (right-top), 16 (right), 17 (right-top & middle),
    28 (top), 31 (top & bottom)
Peter Crabtree: pages 23 (right-top), 26 (bottom)
Bruce Curtis: pages 8 (hockey & baseball), 14 (top)
M. Julian Baum: page 14 (middle-right)
Royalty-Free/CORBIS/MAGMA: page 26 (top)
Other images by Digital Stock, Corbis Images, PhotoDisc,
Adobe, Image Club Graphics/Studio Gear, Image 100

Illustrations
All illustrations by Bonna Rouse except the following:
Katherine Kantor: border (3rd, 4th & 8th images),
    page 3 (top left & right), 11, 19, 25 (top)
Barbara Bedell: front cover (baseball glove)
Trevor Morgan: page 23

Crabtree Publishing Company

www.crabtreebooks.com   1-800-387-7650

PMB 16A	612 Welland Avenue	73 Lime Walk
350 Fifth Avenue	St. Catharines	Headington
Suite 3308	Ontario	Oxford
New York, NY	Canada	OX3 7AD
10118	L2M 5V6	United Kingdom

Cataloging-in-Publication Data
Smithyman, Kathryn
  Active kids / Kathryn Smithyman & Bobbie Kalman.
    p. cm. -- (Kid power)
  Includes index.
  Provides directions for easy-to-do activities to increase strength,
endurance, and flexibility while having fun.
  ISBN 0-7787-1253-2 (RLB) -- ISBN 0-7787-1275-3 (pbk.)
  1. Physical fitness for children--Juvenile literature. [1. Physical fitness.
2. Exercise.] I. Kalman, Bobbie. II. Title. III. Series.
  RJ133.S58 2003
  613'.0432--dc21
                                                    2003002109
                                                    LC

CONTENTS

BEING HEALTHY

What does being healthy mean? You may think it simply means not being sick, but there's more to good health than that. Good health involves your body, your mind, and your feelings. It means eating foods that give your body the **energy**, or physical power, it needs to **function**, or work, at its best. It also means getting enough sleep so your body can recharge its energy and repair itself. Having some physical activity each day is essential to good health as well. Your body works best when you move it regularly. Adding even a few activities can make a big difference in how you feel. Being healthy helps you feel good about yourself, and feeling good about yourself helps keep you healthy.

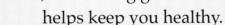

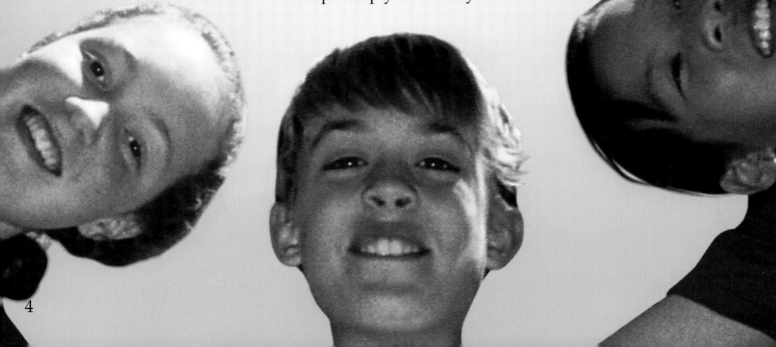

Drink up!

Did you know that more than half of your body is made up of water? To keep your body working properly you need to drink at least six glasses of water every day. You can't live without it for more than four days! If you aren't getting enough water, you may start to feel tired or hungry. These symptoms could indicate that you are **dehydrated**, or in need of water. Spending time outside in hot weather or indoors in heated rooms causes your body to use a lot of water. When you are physically active, you must drink even more water—about one cup of water per half hour of activity—to replace the water your body loses.

Eat well

Your body also needs plenty of **nutritious** food every day. Foods such as **whole grains**, vegetables, fruits, and **lean** meats contain important **nutrients**. Nutrients are substances found in food that fuel your body and give it energy. Most "junk" foods and fast foods are high in sugar and fat and low in nutrients. If you eat more of these foods than nutritious foods, you're keeping your body from getting what it needs. Over time, junk foods can harm your body, so eat these foods only occasionally.

Get active

Getting active is a big part of being healthy. It boosts your brain power, makes you stronger, gives you a more positive attitude, and keeps you from getting sick. Being active and healthy is definitely a good thing!

5

HOW ACTIVE ARE YOU?

About one-third of all young people do not get enough physical activity. Are you active? You could be a lot healthier if you got fifteen minutes of **vigorous**, or highly energetic, activity every day.

Are you fit?

Being **fit** means having a strong, healthy body. When you are fit, your body is able to do the things you want and need it to do. You feel alert and have plenty of energy to perform your daily activities—both at school and at home. When you are fit, you don't get tired doing everyday things such as walking up a flight of stairs. It also means you're able to handle extra "emergency" activities such as running to catch a bus.

Find out!

Are you among the third of young people who aren't active enough? Are you fit or **unfit**? To find out, test yourself against the fitness guidelines in the box on the right. If you can't meet these guidelines, don't give up. Just get up and get active!

Test yourself

Here are some general questions to see if you are fit:

- Can you walk or run a mile (1.6 km) in under ten minutes?

- Can you walk up a flight of stairs without feeling out of breath?

- Can you do about forty abdominal crunches or curl-ups in one minute?

- Can you do a pull-up?

- While sitting with your legs straight in front of you, can you reach your toes?

6

You're worth it!

You can't always judge how fit a person is by how he or she looks. Fit people don't all look the same. Some are thinner, curvier, or have larger muscles than others. Don't compare yourself to your friends or to celebrities. Every person's body is a different shape. The important thing is to feel healthy and strong. Why should you bother being active? You need to bother because you are the most important person in your life, and you deserve to be healthy and happy!

Why should I bother?

Getting active will:

- give you better posture and balance

- give your skin a healthy glow

- help you feel more confident

- make your muscles and bones stronger

- increase your **flexibility** and energy level

- help you maintain a healthy body weight

- reduce the risk of some diseases such as high blood pressure, heart disease, and diabetes, which some people develop as they grow older

- help you form fitness habits that last throughout your life

- help keep your body strong later in your life

- make you feel great!

Couch potatoes

Many young people spend several hours a day playing video games or sitting in front of a television or computer. Although there is nothing wrong with these activities, spending too much time doing them can prevent you from being fit. Try to balance your inactive time with activities such as walking, running, or swimming—anything that gets you moving!

7

WHERE TO START

Getting fit begins with the decision to be more active. Start by thinking of activities you like to do. Doing things you enjoy is the best way to stay **motivated**.

It's okay if you enjoy only one or two activities. Choose an activity you think is fun, such as riding your bike, and do it more often. You're on your way!

One step at a time

You may not realize how much fun you can have being active. This book will help you get started. You may be tempted to start many activities at once, but sticking to them could be a problem. If you're starting to get active, take it one step at a time. Taking on too many activities too quickly may make you feel overwhelmed, and you might be tempted to give up.

Add new activities

To be fit, you must be active more days than you are not. Are you active only occasionally? If you are active during only one season, you will lose your fitness level during the rest of the year. Try some new activities to keep your body moving throughout the year!

Jumping rope is a great physical activity that can be done almost anytime or anywhere.

You may enjoy planned activities such as golf…

…or activities you can do anytime, such as going for a walk.

In-line skating is an activity you can do alone or with friends.

9

THE INSIDE STORY

Your body is an amazing machine! It is made up of many parts that work together as a unit. There are several systems in your body, each with a different purpose. Your **central nervous system**, for example, carries messages between your brain and the rest of your body. Your **respiratory system** controls your breathing and moves oxygen to every part of your body. No system in your body works on its own, however. If one system works poorly, the others will be affected and begin to break down.

The powerhouse

Your body is powered by your **cardiovascular system**. "Cardio" means "heart" and "vascular" refers to your lungs and blood vessels, so your cardiovascular system is made up of your heart, lungs, and blood vessels. Your lungs take in air, which contains the oxygen your body needs. Your lungs are filled with blood vessels that **absorb**, or take in, the oxygen, making your blood **rich**, or filled, with oxygen. Your heart beats **continuously**, or without stopping, to pump the oxygen-rich blood throughout the network of blood vessels that feeds the muscles in your body.

A strong and healthy body will help you enjoy yourself when you're playing sports such as tennis.

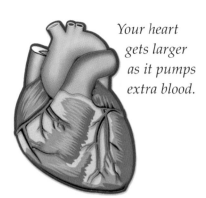

Use the power

Your heart is a muscle that pumps blood throughout your body. When you are resting, your heart beats about 100,000 times a day. When you are active at a continuous, moderate **pace**, or speed, your muscles need more oxygen. Your heart responds by beating harder and faster to pump more blood, which carries the extra oxygen that your muscles need.

Your heart gets larger as it pumps extra blood.

Get outside as often as possible so you can breathe fresh air into your lungs.

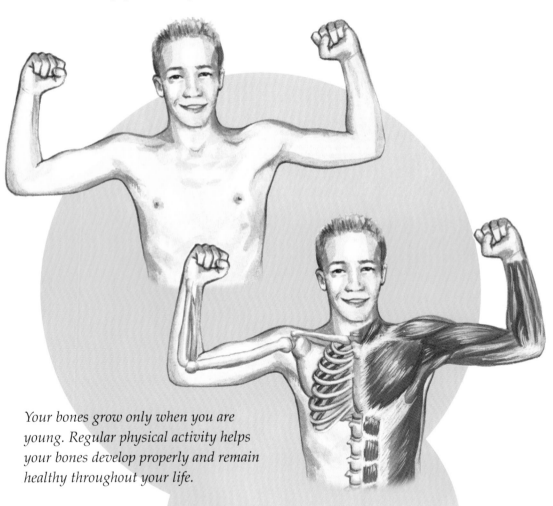

Your bones grow only when you are young. Regular physical activity helps your bones develop properly and remain healthy throughout your life.

Try some tumbling to get your heart pumping faster.

Muscles make you move

Your body is supported by a skeleton of bones. Your bones are attached to muscles. Muscles move your bones in order to move your body. Your muscles work only when they are "fed" by oxygen, which is carried to them by your blood. Some of your muscles are working all the time—even while you sleep!

Being active in a variety of ways helps you get and stay fit.

11

THE BUILDING BLOCKS

To be truly fit, you must exercise your heart and all the muscles in your body. There are three types of activities you need to do: cardiovascular activities, flexibility activities, and strength activities.

"Cardio" activities

Cardiovascular activities get your body moving, which makes your heart beat faster. Walking, running, swimming, and cycling are excellent "cardio" activities because they make you move a lot of muscles at the same time. Any activities that involve running, such as soccer, tennis, or tag, are also good for your heart.

Flexibility

When you are flexible, you are able to move your limbs through a full **range of motion**. For example, if you can swing your arm from your shoulder in a large, complete circle, it means your shoulder has a full range of motion. Flexibility exercises also stretch your muscles so they are not too tight. When you are young, you are naturally flexible, but as you get older, you must work at staying flexible. This girl is stretching her legs and sides.

Strong muscles

Muscle-building activities increase your strength and **endurance**. Having endurance means your muscles don't get tired quickly. For example, while hiking, your legs must be strong enough to carry you to the end of the trail. Your muscles must be strong enough to move your body weight as you do everyday activities such as climbing stairs. This boy's chest and shoulder muscles are strong enough to lift and roll a bowling ball.

Equally important

You need to do all three types of fitness activities to get your whole body fit. The only way to exercise your cardiovascular system is to do cardiovascular activities such as running or dancing. To increase flexibility, you need to stretch your body. Strength-building activities, however, are not always separate activities. Some cardiovascular activities also build strength because when you do them, you are carrying your body weight.

Put on some music and dance for a fun cardiovascular workout.

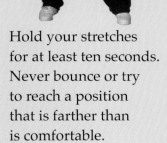

Hold your stretches for at least ten seconds. Never bounce or try to reach a position that is farther than is comfortable.

Hiking is a cardiovascular activity as well as a strength-building activity for the leg muscles. The added weight of the backpack gives this girl a muscle-building workout. If she stretches her body after her hike, she will have done a complete workout.

Walking uphill exercises your heart, and carrying a snowboard strengthens your arm muscles.

13

GET MOVING

To exercise your cardiovascular system, you must move quickly and continue to move for at least fifteen minutes. Moving this way makes your muscles demand more oxygen. You breathe faster and your heart beats harder to pump extra oxygen-rich blood to your muscles. Since these activities increase the amount of oxygen in your body, they are also called **aerobic** activities. Aerobic means "with oxygen."

WHEN YOU
TAKE PART
IN REGULAR
PHYSICAL
ACTIVITY...

... you can do more physical activity.

... your heart gets stronger.

... your other body systems use oxygen more efficiently.

GETTING FIT IS A CYCLE!

... your stronger heart pumps more blood.

... your muscles work better.

... your blood carries more oxygen to your muscles.

Slow and steady

At first, you may not be able to do an activity at a brisk pace for as long as fifteen minutes. Don't give up! Start at a pace that you can handle and move for at least ten minutes. When you can do that activity for at least fifteen minutes, increase your pace. If you can't run for fifteen minutes, for example, walk briskly for ten minutes and then work up to fifteen minutes. You will soon be able to run for fifteen minutes.

Take your pets for brisk walks.

*When you're not able to go outside, find ways to get active indoors. Jumping on a **rebounder**, or mini trampoline, is a great way to get—and stay—active. Moving your arms while you jump or jog on the rebounder will get your heart pumping harder.*

How long can you keep your hula hoop spinning?

Instead of staying inside, go to a public pool on a summer day.

GET FLEXIBLE

Stretching your body helps it become more flexible, and good flexibility helps prevent muscle injuries. Whenever you stretch, use slow, gentle movements, breathe in a natural rhythm, and stay relaxed.

Stretch them all

Flexibility exercises don't necessarily stretch every part of your body, so it is possible to have good flexibility in your legs and poor flexibility in your shoulders. To improve your overall flexibility, you need to do a variety of stretches using different parts of your body. Many muscles come in pairs, so you need to stretch both muscles in a pair. If you stretch the front of your leg, for example, you must also stretch the back of your leg. Examples of stretches for the front and back of your legs are shown on the opposite page.

Being flexible is key to being fit. If you are not flexible, your muscles will not move your body well.

This wrist stretch is a good one to do before any activity involving your arms. It's also a good stretch to use when you're working at a computer.

16

Good balance

Stretching, reaching, and bending improve your posture and balance. As you hold each position, you are working the small muscles in your **torso** that give you good posture. To do balance exercises, you should keep your back straight and hold your stomach muscles tight. This position also improves your posture.

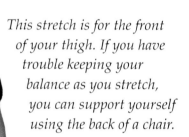

Good posture helps you with activities such as Hackey Sack.

Your muscles can get tight just from sitting! This stretch releases tension in your lower back and shoulders.

This stretch is for the front of your thigh. If you have trouble keeping your balance as you stretch, you can support yourself using the back of a chair.

This position stretches your inner thighs and lower back. Keep your back straight and don't tuck your chin in toward your chest.

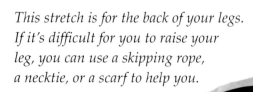

This stretch is for the back of your legs. If it's difficult for you to raise your leg, you can use a skipping rope, a necktie, or a scarf to help you.

This is a great stretch for your calf muscles. Keep your back straight and your heels on the floor.

17

GET STRONG

Without muscles, you would not be able to move. You need strong muscles to climb, run, swim, and jump. Strong muscles give you the strength and endurance you need for all kinds of activities. Muscle-building activities are those that make your muscles work against some kind of **resistance**, such as pushing open a heavy door or moving your body in water. Muscular-endurance activities work your muscles over and over in the same way.

Swimming is an excellent overall muscle builder because you work all your muscles as you push against the resistance of water.

Crunches (shown left) and pushups (shown below) are two of the best exercises for building strength in your upper body.

Muscle specifics

Strength and endurance activities build only the muscles they use. For example, pushups do not strengthen your legs because you are not using your legs to push your body off the ground. Squats work your legs, but they do not work your arms. You need to target different areas if you want all your muscles to be strong.

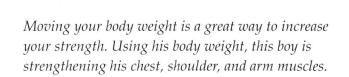

Moving your body weight is a great way to increase your strength. Using his body weight, this boy is strengthening his chest, shoulder, and arm muscles.

18

Choosing the right weight

It is not difficult to determine how much weight you should be lifting. The weight should be light enough that you can lift it 30 times—or do 30 **repetitions**. Do not do 30 lifts at once, however. Do the lifts in three **sets**, or groups, of ten repetitions. After the last set of ten repetitions you should feel as if you have worked very hard. Doing a lot of repetitions will not hurt your growing muscles. Increase the amount of weight you lift only when you are not tired after three sets of ten repetitions.

Lunges build strength in the legs and buttocks.

If you don't have weights, you can lift books or soup cans. Keep your movements slow and steady.

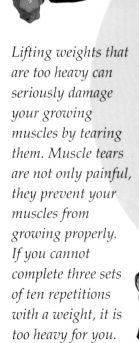

Lifting weights that are too heavy can seriously damage your growing muscles by tearing them. Muscle tears are not only painful, they prevent your muscles from growing properly. If you cannot complete three sets of ten repetitions with a weight, it is too heavy for you.

Always keep the amount of weight you lift on your right side even with the weight on your left side. If, for example, you can lift eight pounds (3.6 kg) with your left arm and five pounds (2.2 kg) with your right arm, stay at five pounds (2.2 kg) on both sides until your right arm catches up.

Rock climbing is a challenging strength-building activity that you can do year-round.

19

WARMiNG UP

Before you get active, you need to warm up your body. Warming up increases the amount of blood that flows to your muscles and your heart—your muscles actually get warmer! Warming up your muscles helps prevent them from being injured. A good warm-up gets your entire body moving. Your goal is to raise your body temperature and cause your heart to beat a little faster. Jogging lightly or walking while moving your arms are good warm-ups for all activities. If you are going to be active for 30 minutes, plan to spend between five and ten minutes warming up. If your activity will be longer, you need a longer warm-up.

Doing a few inner thigh stretches helps this girl prepare her legs for a game of badminton.

Move like you'll move

The best warm-up for any physical activity is simply doing the activity at a slower pace. To prepare for a game of golf, for example, swing your club gently several times to warm up your chest, back, shoulder, and arm muscles. Think about the activity you will be doing and which muscles need to be warmed up.

Limber up

Stretching is also part of warming up, but stretch only after you have warmed up. Stretching is especially important for activities that involve sudden changes in direction, such as soccer, football, and hockey. Do standing warm-up stretches so your heart doesn't slow down too much while you're not moving.

This hockey player skated around the rink a few times to warm up. Now he is using his hockey stick to stretch the front of his shoulders.

COOLING DOWN

When you finish any physical activity, you should spend ten to fifteen minutes cooling down. Walking is the best way to cool down after most physical activities. Walking for several minutes allows your body temperature and breathing to return gradually to normal. To cool down after activities such as cycling, in-line skating, skiing, or paddling a canoe, simply continue the activity at a slower pace. After you have cooled down, you should do some stretches. They can be the same standing stretches you did during your warm-up, but you can also add different stretches. Be sure to stretch all the muscles you used during your activity.

This shoulder stretch is a good one to do before and after activities that use your arms. It can also relieve tension that builds up in your shoulders during the day.

After working hard, do not just stop! You need to slow your pace gradually to give your body a chance to cool down. When your breathing has slowed, continue your cool-down with some stretches, such as this stretch for the back of the legs. You're less likely to be stiff and sore if you cool down immediately after physical activity.

This stretch is good to do after activities that use your legs. It stretches the front of your legs and hips and helps keep you from getting stiff.

You can work with a partner to stretch your lower back and your inner thighs. Hold the stretch for ten seconds.

SAFETY GUIDELINES

It is important to stay safe when you're physically active. Wear all the recommended safety gear, such as a helmet, pads, and guards, for the activities you choose. You must also keep your equipment—such as your bicycle or in-line skates—in good working order. If you do not know how to maintain your equipment, take it to a sporting-goods store or repair shop to be checked.

For fast-moving activities or those that involve contact, such as in-line skating, hockey, and lacrosse, you must wear a helmet to protect your head. The strap should fit snugly under your chin.

Wear clothing that is appropriate to your activity. For example, cyclists should avoid wearing baggy pants that could get caught in the chains of their bikes.

Many activities require specific safety equipment. Always wear the appropriate gear, such as elbow pads or wrist guards, to protect all your body parts.

Select footwear that fits you properly. It should be comfortable and should support your ankles.

Muscle soreness

Whenever you begin a new activity—or when you increase the effort you put into an old one—your muscles will likely be sore. Muscle soreness is natural. It feels tight, tender, or stiff. If you are sore before an activity, begin your warm-up anyway. After five minutes, the soreness should go away as blood circulates through your muscles. If you are sore during an activity, slow down to your warm-up pace. The soreness should ease after a few minutes.

Stop if it hurts!

If you feel sharp or continual pain before or during any physical activity, you must stop the activity immediately. Stopping the activity doesn't mean you should stop moving, however. If you are able to walk, it's better to slow down gradually. Ask an adult for help with first aid. Check with your doctor before starting your activity again. If you feel dizzy during or after your activity, walk slowly—moving toward home—and sip some water.

Check your equipment before starting an activity—it can prevent injuries.

Refuel your body

It is important to drink water whenever you exercise, but it is particularly important in dry or hot weather. Hot temperatures make you sweat more when you're exercising, and you must drink water to replace the fluid you lose. Carry a water bottle with you at all times.

Pay attention to your body. You might be dehydrated if you…

- are extremely thirsty
- are extremely hungry
- are unusually clumsy
- cannot concentrate
- are short of breath
- feel lightheaded
- feel extremely hot
- feel extremely tired
- have a dry mouth
- have muscle spasms
- have a headache
- have a weak but rapid pulse
- are breathing rapidly
- have blurred vision

23

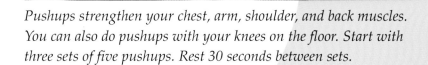

PUTTING IT ALL TOGETHER

You may be involved in physical activities, but you may not be getting the strength training you need to build your muscles. You can do a strength-building workout every other day. Always do a cardiovascular warm-up first—five to ten minutes of walking, running, or skipping will warm up your muscles so they are ready to work. Include two to three activities for your upper body, such as pushups and crunches, and two to three for your lower body, such as lunges.

Do this stretch both as part of your warm-up and as a cool-down stretch after doing pushups. Reach one arm over your head and down your back. With the other hand, pull your elbow back. You will feel the stretch in the back of your arm.

*Skipping gets your heart pumping, and it also helps your balance and **coordination**. You can skip indoors or outdoors—just be sure to clear a space first!*

Pushups strengthen your chest, arm, shoulder, and back muscles. You can also do pushups with your knees on the floor. Start with three sets of five pushups. Rest 30 seconds between sets.

It is important not to pull on your head when you do crunches. Keep your elbows back and your hands resting lightly against the back of your head. Press your lower back against the floor and slowly lift your shoulders off the floor. Start with three sets of five crunches. Rest 30 seconds between sets.

Design your own routine

There are inexpensive pieces of equipment, such as fitness balls or rebounders, around which you can design a routine. A fitness ball is a great tool—bounce on it for a cardiovascular workout or use it for strength and flexibility exercises. The routine shown here consists of three basic moves—bouncing, crunches, and pushups. When you finish these exercises, you should do some upper- and lower-body stretches.

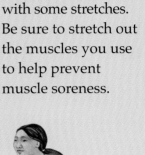

Finish off every routine with some stretches. Be sure to stretch out the muscles you use to help prevent muscle soreness.

Warm up by bouncing lightly on the ball for five minutes. Bounce more vigorously for another ten to fifteen minutes. Moving your arms as you bounce will add to your workout.

Try another way to stretch the back of your leg—pull your weight back as you extend one leg in front with your heel on the floor.

You can do pushups while balancing on your fitness ball! These strengthen your chest, arm, shoulder, and back muscles. Do three pushups, then push back until your feet or knees are on the floor. Rest 30 seconds. Do another three pushups, rest, then finish with three more. Work up to three sets of ten pushups.

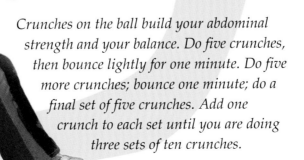

Crunches on the ball build your abdominal strength and your balance. Do five crunches, then bounce lightly for one minute. Do five more crunches; bounce one minute; do a final set of five crunches. Add one crunch to each set until you are doing three sets of ten crunches.

Stretch one arm up while pushing the other arm down to stretch your sides when they feel tight.

iT'S ALL ABOUT EFFORT!

Physical activity doesn't have to be difficult in order to benefit your body. You do not have to be sweating to be exercising, but you should feel like you have worked hard before you finish. Working at a brisk level for ten to fifteen minutes makes your heart and lungs work harder than usual. You'll know you are working hard enough if you are breathing heavily, but not so heavily that you cannot talk. You should be able to talk to someone else—or sing to yourself—while you exercise. After a few workouts, you will learn to listen to your body.

Pushing yourself

At first, everything you do will improve your level of fitness. Over time, however, your body will become used to a level of activity. If you want to continue improving your fitness, you must keep on challenging your body by increasing the effort you put into your activities.

Even riding your bike to a friend's house will improve your fitness level. Take a route with a lot of hills!

26

*As you become **proficient**, or very good, at an activity you will be able to handle a more intense pace—or a more intense activity!*

When you're comfortable with the basics of in-line skating, try skating uphill or around an obstacle course for a more challenging workout. Always be sure to wear the proper safety gear!

Ways to increase effort:
- Continue the activity for a longer period of time.
- Participate in the activity more often.
- Push yourself to work harder while you do the activity.
- Switch to a more challenging activity.

As your level of fitness improves, you may want to try a fast-paced sport such as lacrosse. This sport will test your strength and endurance and give you a great cardiovascular workout!

STAYING MOTIVATED

Once you are more active, you will likely want to try a greater variety of activities. This interest is natural. You will find that it is easier to move your body. You'll probably also have more confidence in trying new sports or exercises. You may find, however, that you need ideas to stay motivated. It's very important to stay motivated because you only receive the benefits of fitness when you **sustain**, or continue, your physical activities.

Count on your friends

Being part of a group may be the motivation you need to be active. If you and your friends often watch television or play video games together, use some of that time to do physical activities instead. Suggest a game of basketball or Frisbee or take up a sport together.

Fun family fitness

Encourage your entire family to become more active. If you support one another, it will become easier for everyone to stay involved. You may decide as a family to watch less TV. This decision may free up a half hour or more to be active. Have a family meeting and decide on some activities your whole family will enjoy doing.

At school

Decide to be active during your recess and lunch breaks at school. If you stand around on the playground with your friends, encourage everyone to take a walk around the school yard. You could also gather a group of classmates to play a game. Find out if your teacher is interested in planning regular school play days.

Sledding is a fun way to spend a winter day with your friends. Did you know it also provides a great workout? Pulling your sled back up the hill exercises your arms, legs, and heart.

28

Cross-training

One way to stay motivated is to get involved in a number of different activities. If you have choices about activities you can do, it will be easier to stay active in poor weather or during different seasons. **Cross-training** is a fitness term for being active in a variety of ways.

Variety is healthy

Your body is healthiest when you mix up your activities. Soccer, swimming, and hiking are all cardiovascular activities, but they move your body in different ways. Swimming, for example, involves a lot of shoulder and arm movement, whereas hiking involves continuous leg movement. Playing soccer requires short bursts of activity, whereas cross-country running needs a steady effort. If you do only one type of activity most of the time, you are using the same muscles over and over again. If you are using your muscles in different ways, however, you will prepare your body for any type of movement. You'll be less likely to be injured by new movements.

Hiking and camping are activities your whole family can enjoy!

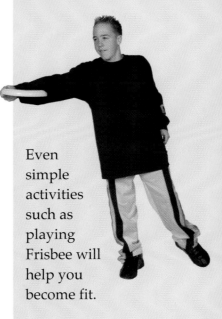

Even simple activities such as playing Frisbee will help you become fit.

Team sports such as relay racing are good ways to meet friends!

29

TAKING THE NEXT STEP

After several weeks of being active, you'll begin to notice changes in your body. You'll feel less out of breath when you walk up a flight of stairs. If you can run up the stairs when you couldn't before, good for you! As your physical activity increases and your fitness level improves, you will notice positive changes in your health and general well-being.

Benefits of fitness

- Do you think about your posture more often? Remember to tighten your abdominal muscles to help you sit, stand, and walk with a straight back.

- Do you find it easier to concentrate at school? Being active helps you to think more clearly.

- Do you sleep better or feel more rested when you wake up? Activity during the day helps your body rest more soundly at night.

All these positive things happen to your body when you get active and stay active!

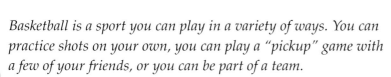

Basketball is a sport you can play in a variety of ways. You can practice shots on your own, you can play a "pickup" game with a few of your friends, or you can be part of a team.

Feeling better about yourself

Some of the results you get from exercise are easy to see. The most important benefits happen inside your body, however. Exercise does amazing things for your mind. When you exercise, your body releases **endorphins**, which are natural painkillers. Endorphins help you deal with stress and make you feel good about yourself. You'll feel more clear-headed and calm when you make physical activity part of your day. Endorphins not only make you feel good, they also strengthen your **immune system**. Your immune system works inside your body to protect you from infections and illnesses.

Eating well

- Never skip breakfast!
- Drink plenty of water, even when you are not working out.
- Choose a variety of foods each day.
- Choose whole-grain foods such as whole-wheat bread, rather than foods made with **refined** flour. Whole-grain foods have more nutrients.
- Eat fresh fruits and vegetables every day. Try to eat some of them raw.
- Cut down on sugar, fat, and **processed foods**. Processed foods come in packages and usually have long lists of ingredients. Many nutrients have been removed from processed foods.
- Read the labels on processed foods to learn what you are really eating.
- Eat at fast-food restaurants less often.

Find out more

If you're interested in finding more activity ideas or information about fitness for kids, check out these websites:

- http://kidshealth.org
- http://www.cahperd.ca/calc
- http://www.fitnessandkids.com
- http://fitness.gov/challenge/challenge.html

GLOSSARY

Note: Words that have been defined in the book may not appear in the glossary.

cardiovascular system The heart, lungs, and blood vessels working together to circulate oxygen throughout the body

central nervous system The brain, spinal cord, and nerves working together to send messages that control the body's systems

coordination Smooth movement among groups of muscles

endurance The ability to continue activity for a long period of time

energy The power to work or do things

fit Able to meet the basic standards of cardiovascular endurance, flexibility, and muscular strength and endurance

flexibility The ability to bend the body easily into various positions

lean Containing little or no fat

motivate To move to action

nutritious Containing ingredients that promote healthy growth and development of the body

range of motion The amount of movement a limb has at its joint

refined Describing food that has been processed to remove coarse parts, or grains

repetition The motion of lifting and lowering a weight one time

resistance A force that slows or stops a motion

respiratory system The organs that carry oxygen into the body and then transport it to the blood

torso The human body excluding the head and limbs

unfit Unable to meet the basic standards for fitness

whole grains Breads and cereals that have not been refined

INDEX

1 2 3 4 5 6 7 8 9 0   Printed in the U.S.A.   2 1 0 9 8 7 6 5 4 3